I0813154

XTREME HORROR LAB
THE SCIENCE OF
GHOSTS
A&D Xtreme
An imprint of Abdo Publishing
abdobooks.com
RUBY DANIELS

TAKE IT TO

THE XTREME!

GET READY FOR AN EXTREME ADVENTURE! THE PAGES OF THIS BOOK WILL TAKE YOU INTO THE SPOOKY WORLD OF UNEXPLAINED PHENOMENA. WHEN YOU HAVE FINISHED READING THIS BOOK, TAKE THE XTREME CHALLENGE ON PAGE 43 ABOUT WHAT YOU'VE LEARNED!

ABDOBOOKS.COM
Published by Abdo Publishing, a division of ABDO, PO Box 398166, Minneapolis, Minnesota 55439.

Printed in the United States of America, North Mankato, MN.
052024
092024

Design: Kelly Doudna, Mighty Media, Inc.
Production: Mighty Media, Inc.
Editor: Jessica Rusick
Cover Photograph: rosinka79/Adobe Stock
Interior Photographs: Alexander Blaikley/Wikimedia Commons, pp. 30–31; bonciutoma/Adobe Stock, pp. 42, 45 (top right); DanielFreyr/Shutterstock Images, pp. 38–39; Dave/Adobe Stock, p. 45 (top middle); David Franklin/Adobe Stock, p. 45 (polaroid frames); Elaine Thompson/AP Images, pp. 34–35; Etienne Gaspard Robertson/Wikimedia Commons, pp. 14–15; Goldilock Project/Shutterstock Images, pp. 40–41; Harry Wedzinga/Adobe Stock, p. 45; Inate/Shutterstock Images, pp. 24–25; Jastrow/Wikimedia Commons, p. 12; JEJordan/Shutterstock Images, pp. 18–19; Juiced Up Media/Shutterstock Images, pp. 28–29; Kozlik/Shutterstock Images, pp. 16–17; Lario Tus/Shutterstock Images, pp. 4–5; Library of Congress, pp. 17, 20–21, 22–23; MarinaP/Shutterstock Images, pp. 36–37; Nick Brundle Photography/Shutterstock Images, pp. 10–11; Raggedstone/Shutterstock Images, pp. 8–9; Rémi Henri Joseph Delvaux/Wikimedia Commons, pp. 26–27 (portrait); rosinka79/Adobe Stock, p. 1; Triff/Shutterstock Images, pp. 26–27 (blackboard); vchal/Shutterstock Images, pp. 32–33; Vitalez/Adobe Stock, p. 45 (top left); Yoyok Langgeng/Shutterstock Images, pp. 12–13; Zvonimir Atletic/Shutterstock Images, pp. 6–7
Design Elements: Dominik Hladik/Shutterstock Images (moon); nikiteev_konstantin/Shutterstock Images (curves); pixelparticle/Shutterstock Images (stars); pixssa/Shutterstock Images (stretchy circle)

LIBRARY OF CONGRESS CONTROL NUMBER: 2023949612

PUBLISHER'S CATALOGING-IN-PUBLICATION DATA
Names: Daniels, Ruby, author.
Title: The science of ghosts / by Ruby Daniels
Description: Minneapolis, Minnesota : Abdo Publishing, 2025 | Series: Xtreme horror lab | Includes online resources and index.
Identifiers: ISBN 9781098293208 (lib. bdg.) | ISBN 9798384912477 (ebook)
Subjects: LCSH: Ghosts--Juvenile literature. | Spirits--Juvenile literature. | Ghosts in popular culture--Juvenile literature. | Science--Juvenile literature.
Classification: DDC 133.1--dc23

TABLE OF CONTENTS

CHAPTER 1

A GHOSTLY SIGHT

It's nighttime. You and a friend are hanging out at her house. You use an old instant camera to take selfies. As one photo develops, you notice something eerie. An old man's face appears to hover in the background! You've never believed in ghosts. But now you're not so sure. Could ghosts actually exist?

CHAPTER 2

TERRIFYING TERMINOLOGY

Medieval Christians believed souls were weighed in the afterlife. This determined whether someone had lived a moral life.

A ghost is a **supernatural** being. Many people believe humans have souls that can exist outside the body. A ghost is the soul of someone who has died. The soul then appears to the living.

Demons are often associated with ghosts.
But they are evil spirits, not human souls.

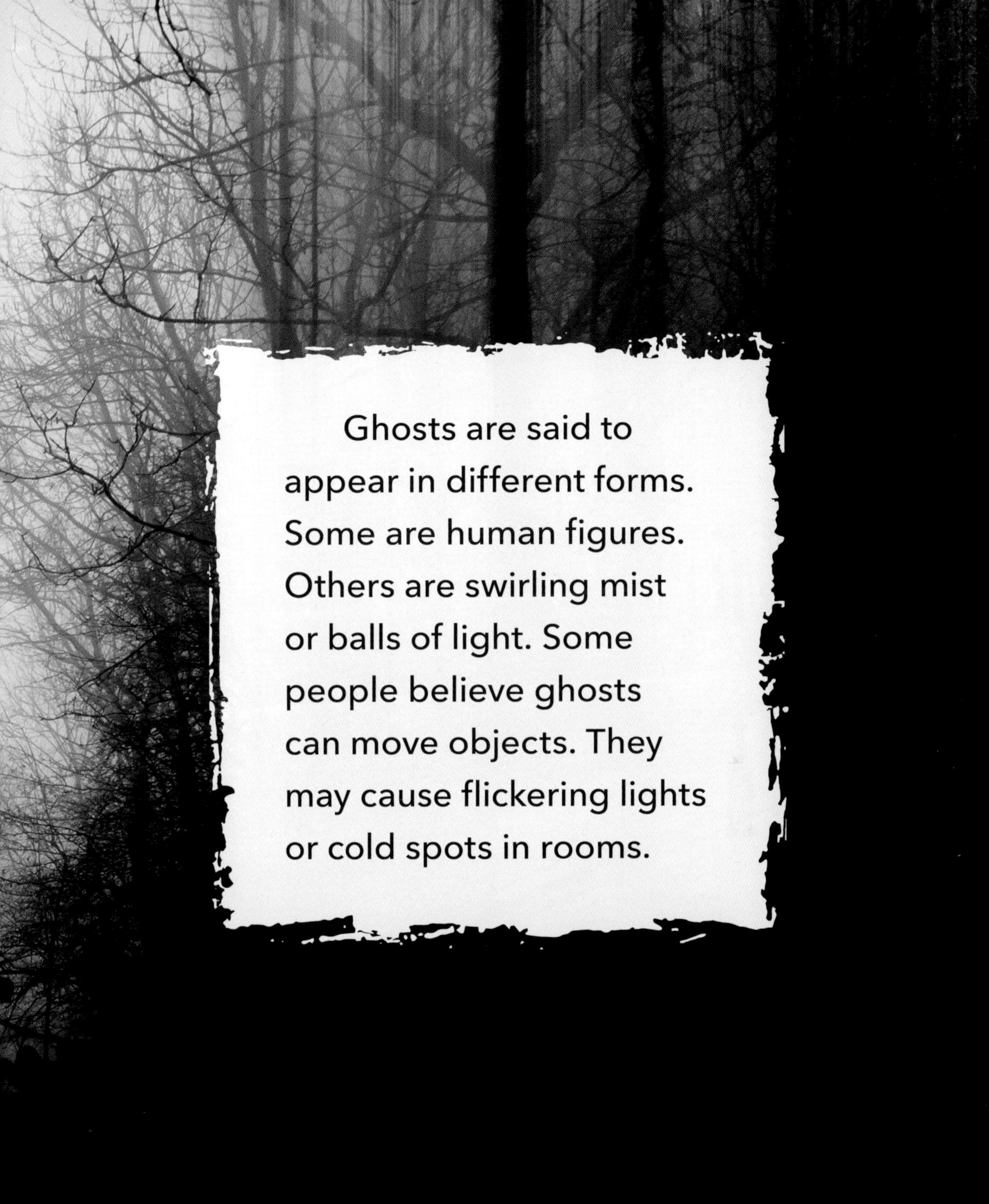

Ghosts are said to appear in different forms. Some are human figures. Others are swirling mist or balls of light. Some people believe ghosts can move objects. They may cause flickering lights or cold spots in rooms.

CHAPTER 3

GHOSTS OF THE PAST

People have believed in ghosts since ancient times. Many cultures believed ghosts were souls that returned from the **afterlife** or refused to go to the afterlife. This was often because of unfinished business or an improper burial. People held elaborate burials to keep the dead in the afterlife.

XTREME FACT

The first known drawing of a ghost was on a Babylonian tablet. It is from 1500 BCE.

Ancient Egyptian pharaohs were mummified before burial to prepare them for the afterlife.

In western folklore, jinn are known as genies. They are powerful beings that can't be seen by humans when in their spiritual form.

Belief in ghosts continued into the **Middle Ages**. These beliefs varied by religion. In Islam, Muslims don't believe the dead can return as ghosts. So, ghost sightings were considered the work of spiritual beings known as jinn. In the early Middle Ages, Christians believed ghosts were tricks of the devil. Later, they thought ghosts needed help from priests to reach heaven.

XTREME FACT

The Hungry Ghost Festival takes place each year in China. Many people believe ghosts can return to Earth during this time.

Wadi Al-Baida, also known as Wadi Al-Jinn, is a valley in Saudi Arabia. Local myths claim that jinn live there.

Phantasmagoria shows were popular in the 1700s and 1800s. Showrunners used mirrors and projectors to make spooky images appear.

The **Enlightenment** of the 1600s and 1700s brought about many scientific advances. Many believed science could prove ghosts' existence. People created theories about how human souls became ghosts. They also collected reports of ghost sightings. But no one was able to prove the existence of ghosts.

CHAPTER 4

SPIRITUALISM & SCIENCE

Beginning in the 1840s, spiritualism spread in the United States and Europe. Spiritualists believed people could communicate with the dead. The movement became popular because of the Fox sisters from New York. They claimed spirits were using knocks to communicate with them. The sisters demonstrated this to paying audiences.

The Fox sisters later admitted they were making the ghostly knocks with their toes.

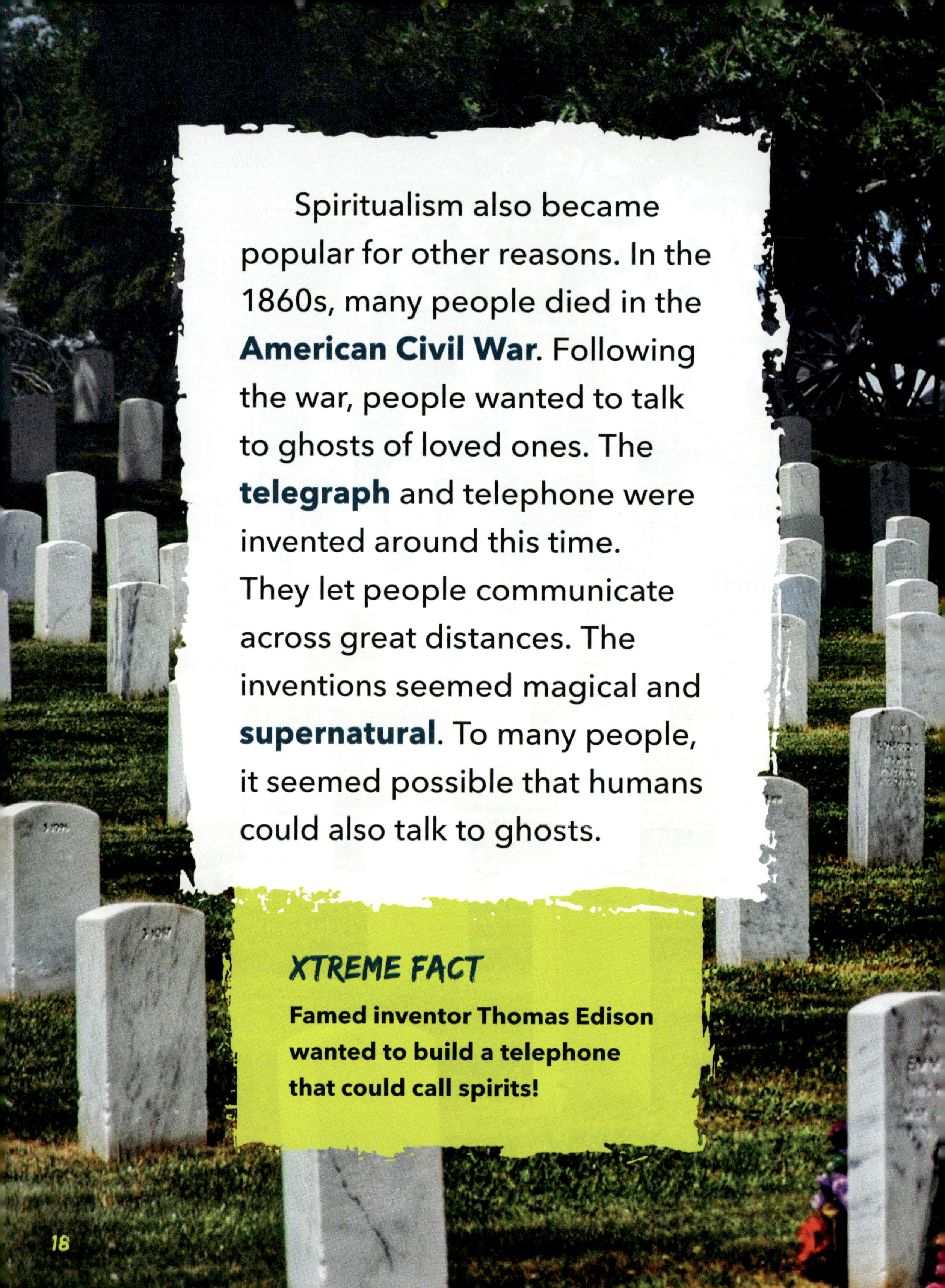

Spiritualism also became popular for other reasons. In the 1860s, many people died in the **American Civil War**. Following the war, people wanted to talk to ghosts of loved ones. The **telegraph** and telephone were invented around this time. They let people communicate across great distances. The inventions seemed magical and **supernatural**. To many people, it seemed possible that humans could also talk to ghosts.

XTREME FACT

Famed inventor Thomas Edison wanted to build a telephone that could call spirits!

The Battle of Gettysburg was the bloodiest battle of the American Civil War. More than 50,000 people were killed, wounded, or captured over three days.

New technology such as the camera and light bulb also seemed **supernatural**. Some people claimed this technology could provide evidence of ghosts.

Spirit photos of the 1800s allegedly showed ghosts hovering near people. But the photos were manipulated to produce that effect.

People claimed blurs in photographs or flickering lights were signs of spirits. It became a popular belief that a ghost's energy could interfere with technology.

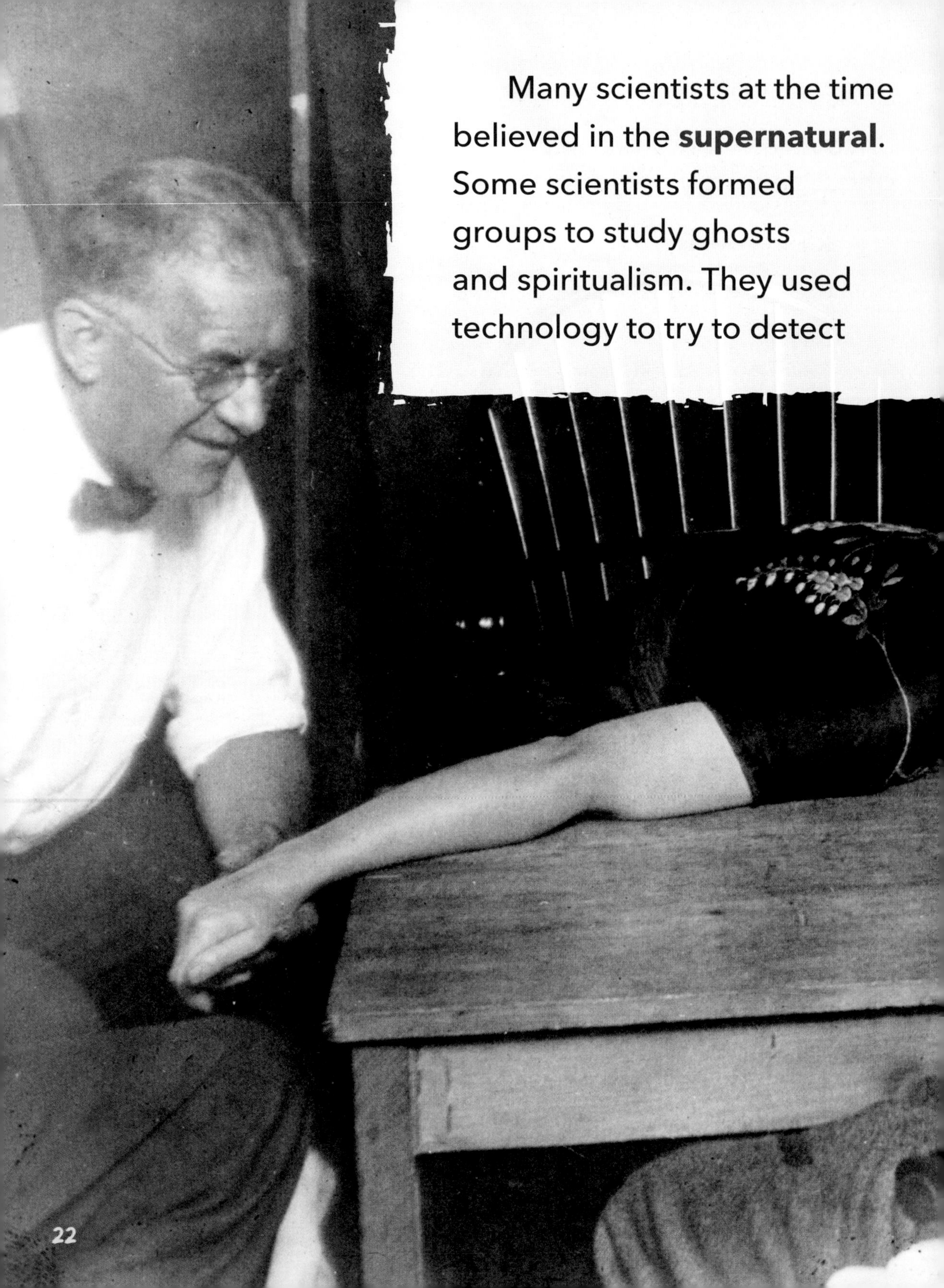

Many scientists at the time believed in the **supernatural**. Some scientists formed groups to study ghosts and spiritualism. They used technology to try to detect ghost activity. Such research uncovered explanations for most ghost sightings. But scientists had some encounters they couldn't explain.

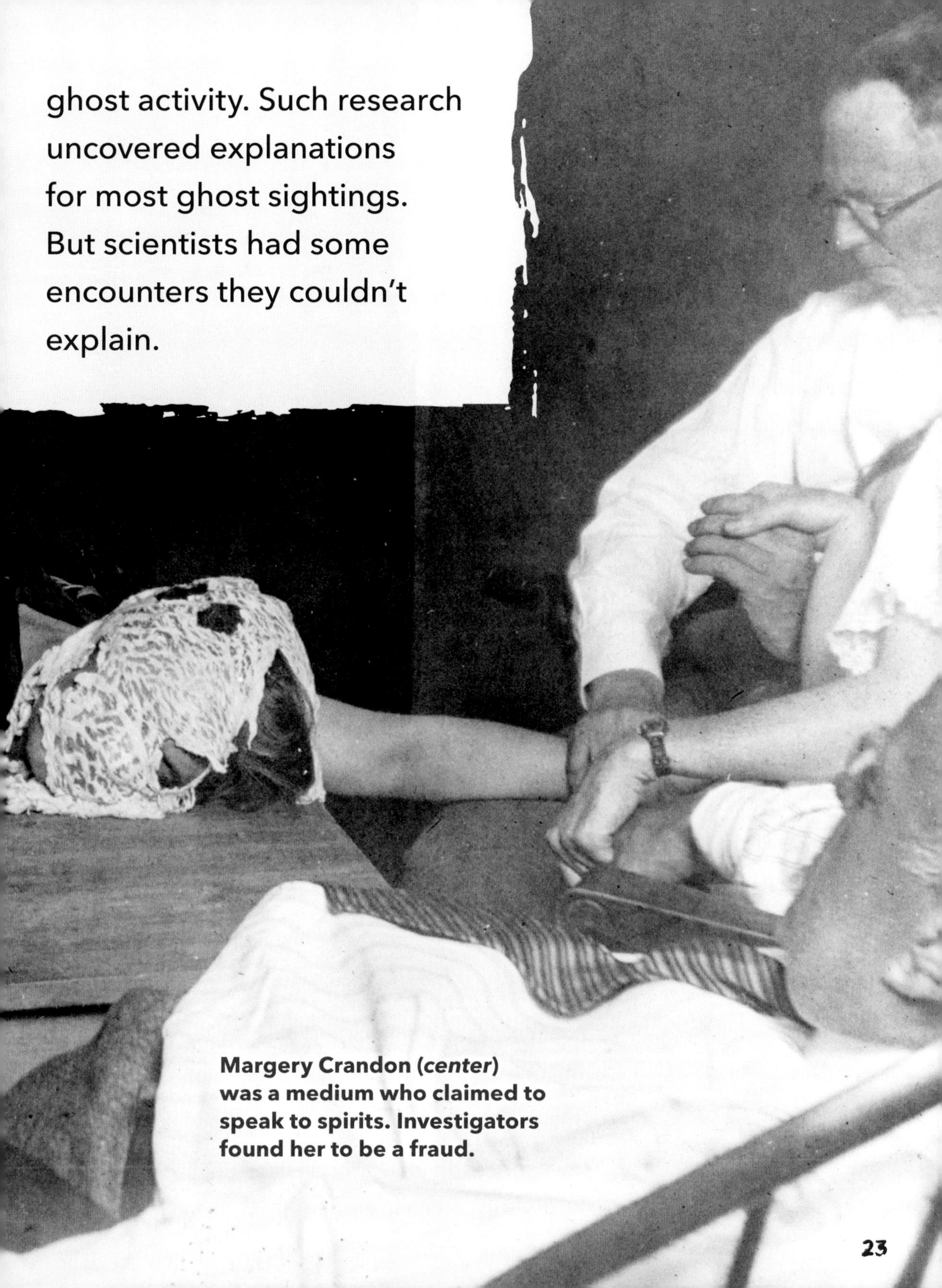

Margery Crandon (*center*) was a medium who claimed to speak to spirits. Investigators found her to be a fraud.

CHAPTER 5

TODAY'S GHOST SCIENCE

The University of Edinburgh in Scotland has a department dedicated to the study of paranormal activity.

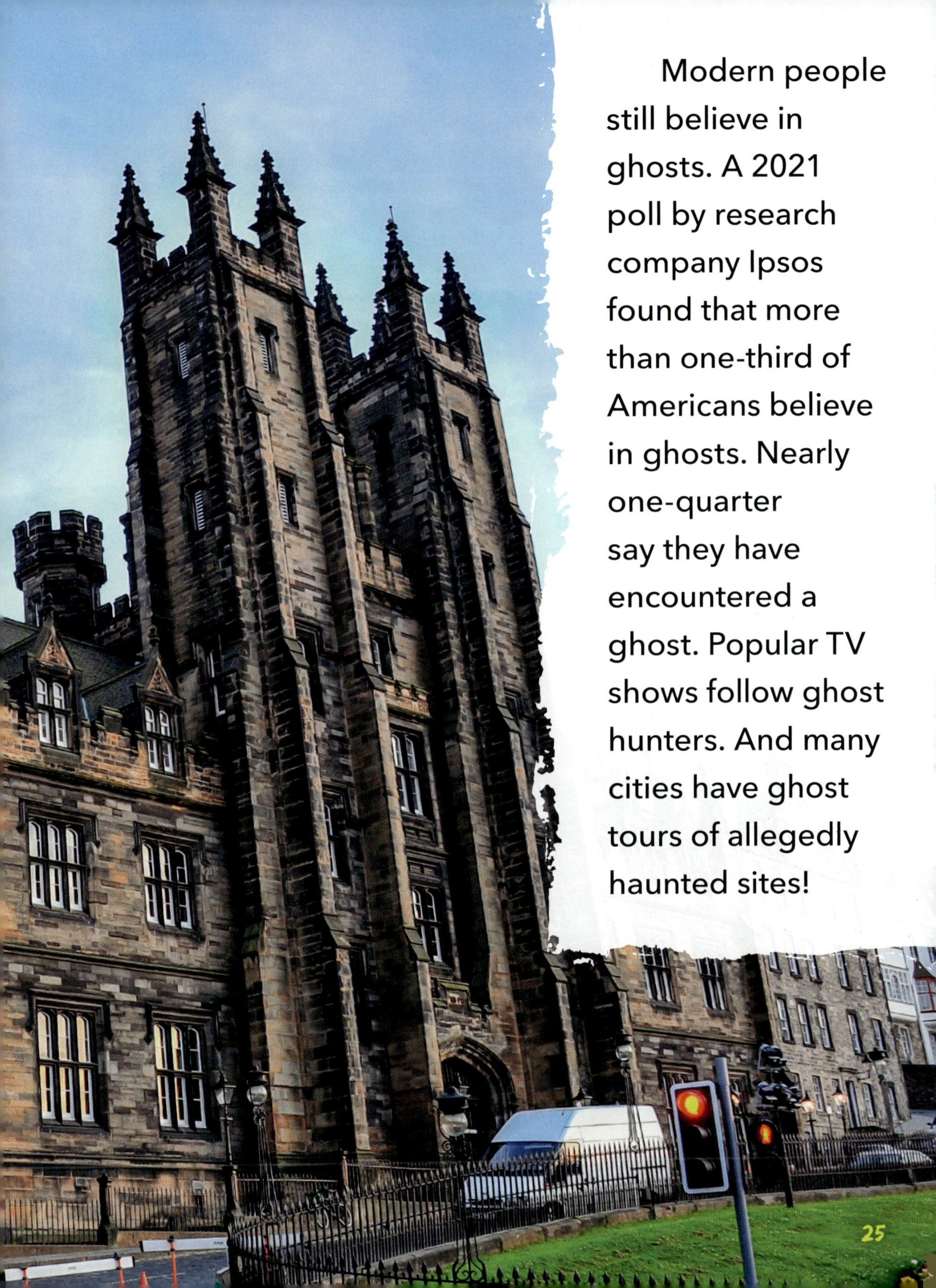

Modern people still believe in ghosts. A 2021 poll by research company Ipsos found that more than one-third of Americans believe in ghosts. Nearly one-quarter say they have encountered a ghost. Popular TV shows follow ghost hunters. And many cities have ghost tours of allegedly haunted sites!

Some people claim the law of **conservation** of energy supports the existence of ghosts. The law states that energy cannot be created or destroyed. People believe a person's energy must turn into a ghost when they die.

The conservation of energy is a law in physics and chemistry. It was first proposed by French physicist Émilie du Châtelet (*inset*).

Modern ghost hunters believe a ghost's energy affects **electromagnetic** fields (EMF). These are invisible energy fields **generated** by electric devices. Some ghost hunting tools detect changes in electromagnetic fields. Others detect changes in temperature and radio waves.

1.5 2.5 10 20+
milliGAUSS(mG)

CHAPTER 6

TERRORS & ERRORS

Scientist Michael Faraday (*at table*) studied electromagnetism in the 1800s. He did not believe ghosts and electromagnetism were connected.

Ghost hunting tools do find evidence of energy changes. However, they are often normal changes. A refrigerator turning on can cause **electromagnetic** field changes. So can faulty wiring. And normal air currents can cause temperature changes.

Ghostly interference with technology can often be explained by the technology itself. Reflections and **rebounding** light can cause accidental "ghost" photography. Flickering lights are often caused by wiring issues or loose light bulbs.

People can manipulate photographs to create "ghosts" with double exposure and digital editing.

Scientist Katrina Spade developed a process to turn human remains into soil.

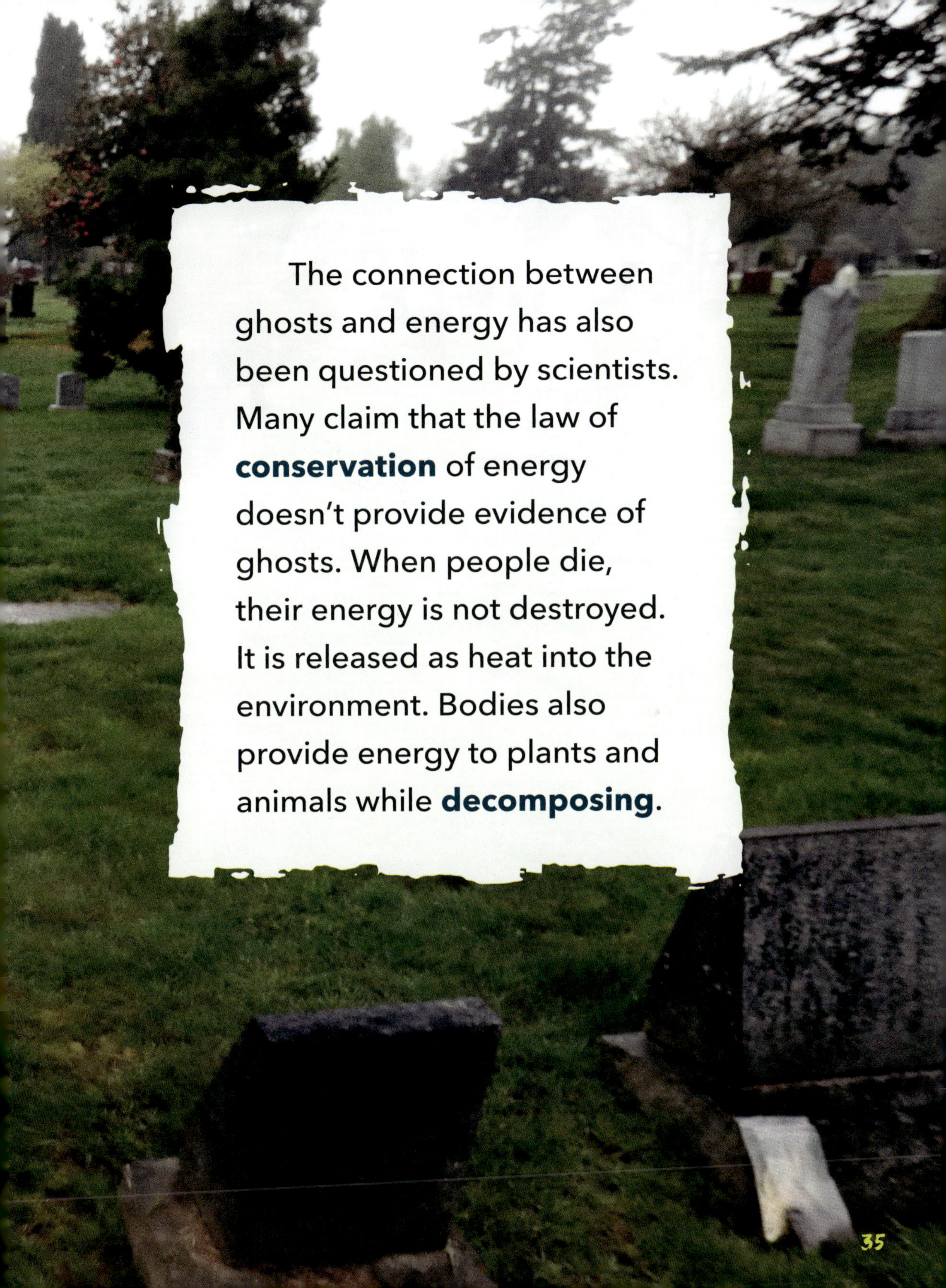

The connection between ghosts and energy has also been questioned by scientists. Many claim that the law of **conservation** of energy doesn't provide evidence of ghosts. When people die, their energy is not destroyed. It is released as heat into the environment. Bodies also provide energy to plants and animals while **decomposing**.

CHAPTER 7

MIND GAMES

Scientists have found different explanations for ghost sightings. Most have to do with the human mind. Many ghost sightings are actually **hallucinations**. Mental illnesses and some drugs can cause hallucinations. Mold, fungus, and **carbon monoxide** can also cause them.

XTREME FACT

Hallucinations can involve any of the five senses. Sound hallucinations are the most common.

Grieving people may have hallucinations of lost loved ones. For some, this can help ease the pain of loss.

Vibrations from appliances or vehicles may also cause ghost sightings. Some vibrations occur at a **frequency** called infrasound. Humans can't consciously hear infrasound. But it can cause fear and affect vision.

Volcanic eruptions can also create infrasound.

The human mind is open to suggestion. People who enter a building they believe is haunted are more likely to see a ghost. Humans also spot patterns where none exist. People may hear words in random noise. They may see faces in ordinary mist.

Humans often see faces in random places and objects.

CHAPTER 8

COULD GHOSTS EXIST?

People have believed in ghosts for centuries. But scientists have been unable to prove that ghosts exist. In the future, improved technology and **techniques** may help uncover more information about ghosts. Until then, people should approach evidence of ghosts with curious but **skeptical** minds.

XTREME CHALLENGE

TAKE THE QUIZ BELOW AND PUT WHAT YOU'VE LEARNED TO THE TEST!

1) What is a ghost?

2) After reading this book, do you believe in ghosts?

3) Why do you think people have believed in ghosts for so long?

4) Why is technology associated with ghosts?

5) What changes do ghost hunting tools try to detect?

GHOST HORROR LAB

See how many of your friends and family members believe in ghosts!

WHAT YOU NEED

- 10 partners
- paper
- pen or pencil

WHAT YOU DO

1. Ask your first partner if they believe in ghosts. Record the response as yes, no, or unsure.

2. Ask the same partner if they have ever encountered a ghost. Record the response as yes, no, or unsure.

3. If this partner answered yes or unsure in step 2, ask for more details about the potential ghost encounter. Record the details.

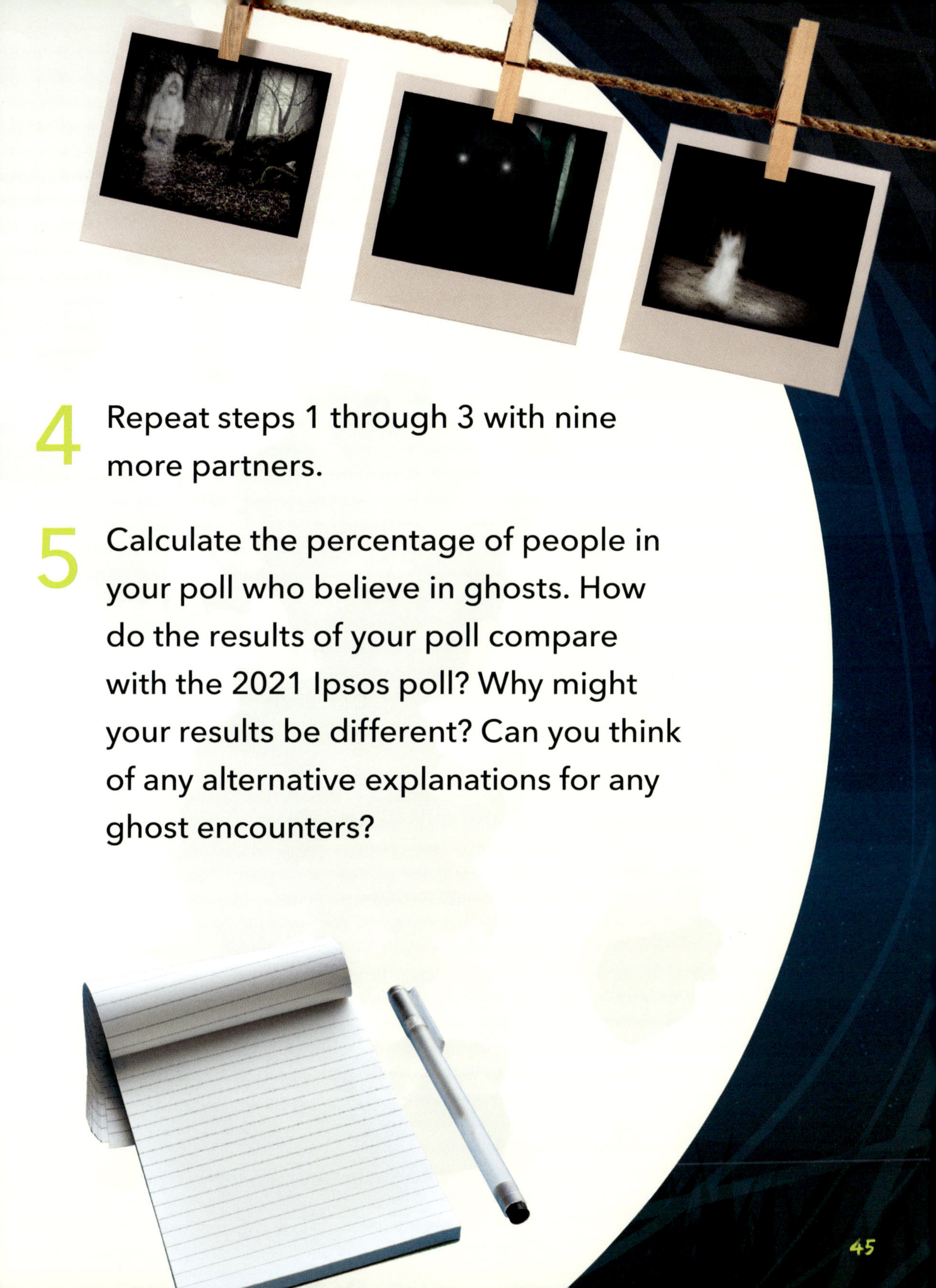

4 Repeat steps 1 through 3 with nine more partners.

5 Calculate the percentage of people in your poll who believe in ghosts. How do the results of your poll compare with the 2021 Ipsos poll? Why might your results be different? Can you think of any alternative explanations for any ghost encounters?

GLOSSARY

afterlife—life after death.

American Civil War—the war between the Northern and Southern states from 1861 to 1865.

carbon monoxide—a colorless, odorless, poisonous gas that forms when carbon is not completely burned.

conservation—the preservation of an amount of something during a chemical reaction or change.

decompose—to break down into simpler parts.

electromagnetic—relating to a magnetic field created by a current of electricity. Electromagnetic fields include radio waves and visible light.

Enlightenment—a movement in Europe in the 1600s and 1700s that stressed the belief in science and logic over tradition.

frequency—the number of waves, such as sound waves, passing a fixed point each second.

generate—to create or produce something.

hallucination—an experience of having heard, seen, smelled, or tasted something that seemed real but was not actually real.

Middle Ages—a period in European history that lasted from about 500 CE to about 1500 CE.

rebound—to bounce back after hitting something.

skeptical—having an attitude of doubt or disbelief.

supernatural—relating to magic, spirits, or other things that cannot be explained by science or nature.

technique—a way of doing something by using special knowledge or skill.

telegraph—a device that uses electricity to send coded messages over wires.

vibration—very small, quick movements back and forth.

ONLINE RESOURCES

To learn more about ghosts, please visit **abdobooklinks.com** or scan this QR code. These links are routinely monitored and updated to provide the most current information available.

INDEX